The Disruptive Power of Blockchain

High-Tech, Finance, and Society

Table of Contents

Chapter 1. Introduction

In this Special Report, we delve into one of today's most pivotal technological breakthroughs: blockchain. Don't let the high-tech terminology intimidate you; we've crafted this report in a way that's relatable and digestible for everyone, regardless of your technical background. As the driving force behind cryptocurrencies like Bitcoin, blockchain's transformative potential extends far beyond finance; it's reshaping entire sectors and challenging societal norms on privacy, trust, and inclusion. So, whether you're intrigued by the promise of a decentralized future or just want to demystify the buzzwords, our report: "The Disruptive Power of Blockchain: High-Tech, Finance, and Society" is your essential guide. It's not just about understanding a technology; it's about being prepared for a revolution. Get ahead of the curve — grab your copy today and embark on this educational journey!

Chapter 2. Understanding Blockchain: From Cryptocurrency to Deeper Applications

Blockchains, at their core, consist of a series of immutable records, known as 'blocks', maintained across a network of computers, dubbed 'nodes'. Each block is connected to its predecessor through a cryptographic hash function, creating a 'chain' — hence the term 'blockchain'. Coupled with its distributed nature, this chain's immutability makes it nearly impossible to alter past transactions without the network detecting it.

2.1. The Mechanics of Blockchain

A primary feature that sets blockchains apart is their decentralized nature. Unlike traditional databases administered by a central authority, these chains consist of distributed ledgers that any computer on the network can access. However, operating in a decentralized fashion doesn't mean chaos and anarchy. In fact, there are tight protocols that must be followed to validate and log new blocks.

Each node in the network carries a replica of the entire blockchain ledger. On the transaction's initiation, nodes work to verify its authenticity. This is done through a process known as 'mining' in blockchain terminology. When miners solve a complex mathematical problem, they add the verified block to the chain, and the initiating party's transaction is considered validated.

2.2. Blockchain and Cryptocurrency: An Inextricable Link

Most notably, blockchain technology serves as the backbone of cryptocurrency, with Bitcoin emerging as its most famous application. Created by an anonymous figure or group dubbed 'Satoshi Nakamoto', Bitcoin presented world-changing potential by proposing an alternative to traditional fiat currency. Using blockchain, Bitcoin transactions are validated and stored on the ledger, providing a clear and transparent history that prevents double-spending and fraud.

Since the debut of Bitcoin, numerous other cryptocurrencies have entered the arena. Ethereum is one such example, introducing the concept of smart contracts into the blockchain layer. Smart contracts function as self-executable contracts with the terms of the agreement written into its code, allowing trustless, automatic execution on the blockchain. This was a revolutionary concept, vastly expanding blockchain's potential applications.

2.3. Moving Beyond Cryptocurrency

The technological invention of blockchains can't be enclosed within financial transactions alone. A compelling case can be made for blockchains in numerous other domains, from supply chain management to healthcare and more. Speaking simplistically, any industry that requires secure recordkeeping, transparency, and/or verification can make use of blockchain technology.

In supply chain management, blockchain can provide real-time tracking of goods, link physical goods to barcodes or digital tags, and monitor compliance. In healthcare, blockchain can streamline patient records, controlling who sees what, when, and ensuring data integrity. It can also be used for verifying the authenticity of medicines — a critical step in countering the widespread issue of counterfeit drugs.

Even in governance, blockchain has a role to play. Voting systems, for instance, can be made more secure, transparent, and immune to tampering with this technology.

2.4. Understanding Decentralized Finance (DeFi)

A recent trend in the blockchain domain is Decentralized Finance or DeFi. In particular, DeFi aims to replace traditional financial services — like lending, borrowing, and trading — with blockchain-based solutions. This way, the need for intermediaries, such as banks and brokers, is eliminated, resulting in faster, cheaper, and more democratic financial services.

The potential implications here are enormous. For individuals living in regions where banking services are substandard or practically non-existent, DeFi could pave the way to financial inclusion, opening new avenues for economic prosperity.

2.5. The Road Ahead for Blockchain

The journey of blockchain technology is still in its early days. While its inroads in cryptocurrency and finance are well-documented, its shakeup of other sectors is only just beginning. As we move further into a digitized world, the need for efficient, reliable, and secure systems to manage and transact information becomes more critical. Blockchain technology, with its inherent security, transparency, and decentralization, is well placed to meet this need.

Nevertheless, like all innovations, blockchain isn't without its challenges. Issues related to scalability, energy consumption, understanding, and adoption remain, and need to be addressed to harness this technology's full potential. However, as we navigate the intricacies of this pioneering technology, it's crucial to keep our minds open to the possibilities it holds. More than a technological breakthrough, blockchain could be the dawn of a new kind of internet — a decentralized, democratic, and transparent one.

As we close this chapter, remember that understanding blockchain is more than deciphering complex terminologies and technological jargon. It's about appreciating a fundamental shift in information management and transactions — a shift that's as much about societal change as it is about digital transformation. This understanding will help us critically approach the numerous applications, benefits, and challenges that blockchain and its derivative technologies promise to bring.

Chapter 3. Demystifying Decentralization: A New Paradigm of Trust

Understanding decentralization begins with comprehending how our traditional systems work. The conventional structure of governance, finance, and even technology is predominantly centralized. Government bodies, banking institutions, data servers— all typically have a focal point or a hub that controls and regulates all operations.

3.1. Centralization Vs. Decentralization

Centralization pools authority and control at a single point. One governing body or entity makes all the decisions, controls the resources, and holds the power. For instance, a traditional bank is a centralized organization. It exercises authority over your money, your transactions, and your account details. It maintains a central server that records all movements in a ledger. In case of a server failure or a security breach, the entire system suffers.

Decentralization, on the other hand, involves spreading out the control, decision-making authorities, and resources over many entities or nodes in a network. A blockchain network is a classic instance of a decentralized system. Here, instead of a single ledger maintained by a central authority, every node in the network has a copy of the entire ledger. Decisions are made based on consensus among nodes, ensuring a democratic process.

3.2. The Significance of Decentralization

If your money is tied up with a centralized bank and it fails, your assets are at significant risk. But in a decentralized network, the failure of one node barely affects the overall system since every other node has a complete copy of the ledger. This brings us to the several merits of decentralization:

1. Resistance to Failures: Since there's no single point of failure, decentralized networks can withstand various issues that would cripple a centralized system.

2. Security: With data scattered across a network and not held in a central hub, hacking attempts are significantly more difficult.

3. Transparency and Trust: Every action is accounted for in a public ledger. This level of transparency fosters trust among participants.

4. Impact on Power Structures: Decentralization wrestles control away from a single entity and puts it into the hands of many individuals.

3.3. The Blockchain Effect

Blockchain technology epitomizes the paradigm shift towards decentralization. It provides us with a new way to handle and store data, without relying on centralized entities. Every block in a blockchain stores a list of transactions, adding onto its predecessors in a linked chain. Updates occur across the entire network, ensuring that all participants have a consistent and complete copy of the ledger.

3.4. Trust in Blockchain

Trust in the blockchain stems from its technical foundation: complex cryptography, network consensus, and decentralization. It doesn't rely on a central authority, but instead trusts the immutability of math and algorithms. Once a transaction is recorded in a block and added to the chain, it is nearly impossible to change that record.

This paradigm has the potential to disrupt traditional sectors like finance, government, and even interpersonal relationships. Businesses, large and small, governmental and non-profits alike, stand to gain from the amplified transparency, security, and consistency offered by blockchain technology. It's more than a technical revolution, it's a new paradigm of trust.

3.5. Are Decentralized Systems Perfect?

While decentralization offers many benefits, it isn't a silver bullet for all societal and technical problems. Decentralized systems face challenges with performance, scalability, governance, and potential misuse. These issues need attention and further research to fully harness the potential of decentralization and make it accessible to the wider mass.

In conclusion, decentralization is more than a technological trend; it is underpinning a new way of structuring systems—be it in finance, regulation, or data storage. As we move further into the digital age, understanding and leveraging the merits and potential of decentralized systems—and blockchain technology, in particular—will become increasingly critical. From undermining established power structures and establishing new models of trust, to bolstering privacy and security, the disruptive power of decentralization is here, and shaping our future.

Chapter 4. The Blockchain Impact: Transforming the Financial Sector

The financial sector has traditionally been characterized by a complex web of intermediaries - banks, credit card companies, and other financial institutions - all indispensable for ensuring the integrity and smooth operation of transactions in a trust-based system. However, with the advent of blockchain, these processes are set for a seismic shift. Harnessing the power of blockchain technology, the infrastructure of the financial world can be significantly simplified, making transactions faster, cheaper, and more secure.

4.1. Tearing Down Intermediaries

At its core, blockchain operates as a 'distributed ledger', a shared record of transactions maintained by a network of computers termed as 'nodes'. Each node operates a copy of the ledger, ensuring transparency and preventing manipulation of financial data. Real-time updates and the irreversible nature of the entries enhance accuracy and reliability.

In a world riding on this new wave of technology, the necessity for intermediaries in financial transactions is significantly reduced. Blockchain renders intermediation redundant, as transactions are validated and recorded across multiple nodes. It improves efficiency and transparency, reduces cost, and offers a higher level of security.

4.2. Faster and More Efficient Transactions

International wire transfers and remittances in the current financial system can take days to process due to the hand-offs between multiple institutions. The conventional system is plagued with delays and is highly centralized, vulnerable to systemic risks and individual points of failure. Blockchain technology provides a faster, more efficient way to send money across borders.

By allowing peer-to-peer transactions in a decentralized network, blockchain expedites the process and substantially cuts down on processing fees. Cryptocurrencies like Bitcoin and Ethereum have showcased this potential, carrying out transactions in minutes rather than days and eliminating interbank fees.

4.3. Reimagining Securities Trading

Often considered an arcane world, the securities trading arena can tremendously benefit from blockchain technology. Currently, the buying and selling of securities involve numerous intermediaries, like the broker, the exchange, clearing houses, and the custodian.

Blockchain technology promises to replace this labyrinthine system with a more streamlined, efficient one. It can simplify the process, allowing securities to be traded with digital tokens in a trustless environment. It can also automate settlement, eliminate reconciliation, and deter fraudulent activities, making financial markets more secure and inclusive.

4.4. Bringing Unprecedented Security

Blockchain's distributed consensus model is what lends it an unprecedented level of security. The records are secure from tampering and revision. Each 'block' contains a unique 'hash' of the previous block, creating a chain of interdependent records. Altering information in a block would require re-hashing of all subsequent blocks, which is virtually impossible given the computational power involved.

Additionally, blockchain technology can protect financial services from cyberattacks. With the data decentralised and stored across many nodes in the network, breaching security becomes significantly more complex.

4.5. Democratizing Finance and Fostering Financial Inclusion

Nearly a third of the world's population lacks access to basic financial services, marginalized by the traditional banking sector's inability to service low-income or remote populations. Blockchain provides a cost-effective solution to this, facilitating financial inclusion.

With digital wallets and peer-to-peer transactions, users can engage with financial services without traditional bank accounts. Blockchain could facilitate microloans, aid distribution, remittances and other financial services, fostering socio-economic empowerment in the underserved regions.

4.6. Reimagining Identity Verification Processes

Identity verification is a long-drawn and complex process in traditional banking systems. The high costs of Know Your Customer (KYC) and Anti-Money Laundering (AML) compliance are a burden. With blockchain, a decentralized and immutable record of identities can be established.

Once an identity is verified on a blockchain, it can be referenced by other parties to quickly and inexpensively confirm a customer's identity, enhancing security while reducing costs for compliance processes.

4.7. The Future Of Blockchain In Finance

While sceptics argue the merits of blockchain and cryptocurrencies, it's clear that they offer compelling advantages over the conventional systems. Ongoing projects at various financial institutions and consortia worldwide are indicative of blockchain's transformative potential in finance.

However, these transformations will not be without challenges. Regulatory uncertainties, cultural shift and technological scalability are significant hurdles to navigate. Notwithstanding these challenges, it is undeniable that blockchain has provided a tantalizing glimpse into a more decentralized, inclusive, efficient, and transparent financial system.

The blockchain revolution reshaping the financial sector is already underway, and the pace of change is breathtaking. The key to harnessing this revolution lies in understanding its potential, embracing the change, and anticipating the implications. Blockchain stands not just as a technological breakthrough, but also as a driver of profound societal change, fostering greater financial inclusion and economic resilience. The impact of blockchain on the finance sector has only just begun. The coming years will unveil the full extent of its transformative power.

Chapter 5. Beyond Bitcoin: The Extended Reach of Blockchain Technology

Blockchain technology shone a spotlight on its potential when it served as the foundation for Bitcoin, the first globally recognized and high valued digital currency. However, the story doesn't end there. The various characteristics and capabilities of blockchain technology extend its scope far beyond Bitcoin and even beyond the financial sector.

5.1. From Financial Transactions to Record Keeping

In essence, blockchain is a secure, transparent, and immutable ledger system. This characteristic makes it suitable for an array of applications where record keeping is a crucial factor. From tracking materials through a supply chain or maintaining educational records, blockchain technology can offer security, accessibility, and trustworthiness to the system.

One novel example of its use beyond Bitcoin is found in the food industry. Walmart has partnered with IBM to use its blockchain program to track the sale of pork in China. Walmart stores record each piece of meat's journey from origin to store onto a blockchain. This record ensures the pork is healthy, ethically sourced, and fresh when customers purchase it at Walmart. The adoption of such a system also drastically speeds up the process of tracing any tainted food products back to their source, going from days to mere minutes.

This application of blockchain demonstrates the technology can provide transparency, increase efficiency, and maintain tamper-proof records, making it increasingly popular in various sectors beyond finance.

5.2. Decentralization in Content Creation

The internet, as we currently know it, is fragmented and controlled by various centralized bodies (like Facebook, Google, etc.), leading to an imbalance of power and monopolization of data. Blockchain technology could shift this centralized internet towards a decentralized model, empowering individual users and content creators more directly.

Steemit, a blogging and social networking platform, rewards its users with its own cryptocurrency for publishing and curating content. This model, driven by blockchain, incentivizes the creation and curation of quality content by its members.

Such a decentralized system promotes fairness, discourages centralization, and could change how the future of the internet and content creation looks.

5.3. Blockchain for Digital Identity Verification

Digital identity verification is becoming increasingly important in our interconnected world. Blockchain offers a prospective solution through its transparent and accessible network. The Estonia government already uses a blockchain called KSI to secure its citizens' health records, tax records, and digital identities.

Utilizing blockchain for digital identities can bypass intermediaries, reduce identity theft, lower the cost of identity verification, and allow users control over their personal data.

5.4. Smart Contracts

Smart contracts are self-executing contracts with the terms of the agreement being directly written into lines of code. Etherium was one of the first platforms to introduce smart contract capabilities, illustrating the diversified usage of blockchain technology.

Smart contracts minimize the need for trusted intermediaries, reduce paperwork, increase transaction speed, and ensure a high level of security. It offers great potential for various sectors from real estate to insurance policymaking.

5.5. Non-Fungible Tokens (NFTs)

Blockchain technology has recently proved instrumental in the creation of non-fungible tokens (NFTs)—cryptographic tokens that represent a unique item or piece of content. More than a trend, NFTs could potentially disrupt the art world by enabling artists to maintain ownership and earn royalties each time their work is sold.

In conclusion, blockchain's potential goes far beyond Bitcoin. Its inherent characteristics of security, transparency, and decentralization offer promising opportunities across various non-financial sectors, leading the way toward a new form of digitized trust and interaction. As the technology continues to evolve, it's likely that innovation will uncover even more applications for blockchain.

Chapter 6. Shaping the Future of Transactions: Smart Contracts

Before delving into the nuts and bolts of how smart contracts operate and how they are transforming the landscape of transactions, it's essential to understand the term itself. A smart contract is a self-executing contract with the terms of the agreement directly written into lines of code. The code and the agreements contained there within exist across a decentralized blockchain network.

6.1. Why Smart Contracts?

Smart contracts were first proposed in the mid-1990s by Nick Szabo, who coined the term. Szabo envisaged that contracts could be converted into computer code and automatically executed once certain predetermined conditions were met. This idea, which was way ahead of its time, struggled to find real-world applications until the advent of blockchain technology.

In a blockchain context, smart contracts are a type of decentralized application (dApp) that operate on a blockchain platform. These contracts are programmatically designed to execute, control, or document events or actions according to the terms of a contract or agreement.

6.2. The Mechanics of a Smart Contract

Every smart contract transaction is visible and validated by the network, using blockchain's key feature of a decentralized ledger.

This means that for a transaction to become valid, it must be approved by multiple nodes within the network. Once the smart contract agreement is embedded into a blockchain, it cannot be altered or amended, thereby ensuring its immunity against tampering.

Smart contracts operate using 'if-then' logic. Essentially, if a certain set of conditions set out within the contract is met, then the contract self-executes and delivers the outcome agreed by the parties. For instance, in a smart contract for a property transaction, the ownership of the house would be transferred as soon as the payment is verified on the blockchain network.

6.3. Smart Contracts and Ethereum

Ethereum – the blockchain designed by Vitalik Buterin - allows developers to build decentralized applications, including smart contracts, on its platform. It's virtual currency, Ether, is not just for peer-to-peer payments but also pays for transaction fees and computational services on the Ethereum network.

Smart contracts on Ethereum are scripted in a language called Solidity. These contracts become a perfect neutral arbiter of a transaction, removing the need for a third party and democratizing transactions of all kinds.

6.4. Use Cases

As smart contracts offer security, automation, speed, accuracy, and cost-effectiveness, they have potential use cases far beyond financial transactions.

1. **Insurance**: In insurance, automated payout conditions in the case of certain events can be outlined in a smart contract. In the occurrence of the specified event, the smart contract is triggered

to process the claim and automatically transfer the claimed amount.

2. **Real Estate**: Real estate transactions can be facilitated by smart contracts. They can automate the transfer of ownership rights of an asset upon receipt of payment. This method eliminates the need for middlemen and substantially reduces the total time and costs involved.

3. **Supply Chain**: In supply chain management, smart contracts can bring in traceability and accountability. They can be used to automate procurement, tracking, and delivery processes based on conditional checkpoints.

6.5. Current Challenges and Future Outlook

As promising as smart contracts are, they're still in a nascent stage and face several barriers to mainstream implementation.

Interoperability is one of the major challenges. As there are many blockchain platforms, each operating with different coding languages and protocols, there is a lack of standardization among smart contracts. Secondly, smart contracts also raise legal uncertainty and regulatory issues. For instance, if a smart contract transaction goes wrong, jurisdiction issues to resolve the dispute can be complex.

However, with continual advancements in blockchain technology, many of these challenges will have solutions in the coming years. Notably, effectively addressing these barriers will be crucial to fully leverage the power of smart contracts and their potential to shape the future of transactions across various sectors.

Despite the obstacles, the future appears bright for smart contracts. They have far-reaching potential in transforming transactions by promoting efficiency, transparency, and trustlessness. As understanding of this technology improves and regulatory frameworks mature, you can anticipate seeing more widespread adoption of smart contracts in a host of applications, both within and beyond the financial sector. This adoption certainly aligns with the overall shift towards a more decentralized future that blockchain technology promises.

Chapter 7. Blockchain and Society: Changing the Rules of Privacy

In the realm of digital privacy, blockchain is emerging as a potential game-changer. It's heralded as a revolutionary tool which, by its very design, aspires to redefine user privacy as we know it. With its decentralized structure and cryptographic features, blockchain technology pushes us to reconsider our conventional understanding and expectations around privacy.

7.1. The Paradigm Shift in Privacy

Blockchain triggers a shift in emphasis from centralized bodies collecting and controlling vast streams of personal data to individuals commanding their own digital information. It flips the established tropes of data and power by decentralizing data control, aligning it more closely with individuals than with centralized corporations or institutions.

Fairly recently, an individual's digital identity was usually managed by centralized data silos owned by large corporations. However, blockchain-based digital identity systems could potentially enable individuals to control their own data, making decisions about whom to share it with and what they should get in return.

Leveraging blockchain's immutability and verifying mechanisms, this new model of identity verification eliminates the need for repeated validation of data by different entities. The ledger-based system on which blockchain operates creates digital "fingerprints" or hashes that are unique to every transaction, hence creating a secure and indelible method for data verification.

7.2. Digital Identity and Self-Sovereign Identity

Much of the excitement around blockchain's impact on privacy centers on the potential for self-sovereign identity. Self-sovereign identity envisages a world where individuals and organizations would have sole ownership of their digital and analog identities.

These identities have the potential to replace the multiple usernames and password combinations we are currently burdened with. We could use a single blockchain-based identity for numerous different applications, drastically simplifying our routines in the digital environment.

Additionally, your digital identity could be used to verify aspects about you without the need to disclose the actual data. For example, a blockchain-based system could verify that you are over a certain age without needing to reveal your actual date of birth, thereby preserving your privacy.

7.3. Privacy and Public Blockchains

An important aspect to clarify is the distinction between privacy and anonymity. Though public blockchains like Bitcoin are often hailed as anonymous, they are better described as pseudonymous. While transactions are not directly linked to users' identities, patterns could be analyzed over time to link a public key with an individual.

Some blockchains offer improved privacy features. For example, Monero uses ring signatures and stealth addresses to hide sender and receiver identities. Another cryptocurrency, Zcash, leverages a cryptographic method known as zk-SNARKs to deliver a greater level of privacy to its users. Yet, these tools are only as effective as their implementation – and they require comprehensive understanding and use by cryptocurrency users to adequately maintain privacy.

7.4. Implications for Societal Norms and Legislation

As with any disruptive technological innovation, blockchain's revolutionary potential in regards to privacy is not without its challenges. These changes are set to pose teething problems to society at large and to regulatory bodies in particular.

Regulations such as the EU's General Data Protection Regulation (GDPR), aimed at protecting individuals' data rights, can be seen in conflict with blockchain. For example, one key issue is the "right to be forgotten," where individuals have the right to get their data erased. This contradicts the main characteristic of blockchain – its immutability.

It will be critical for future laws and regulations related to digital privacy to consider the unique aspects of blockchain technology. This would mean governments and regulatory bodies must evolve along with technology, embracing these new concepts for the potential benefits they can bring to society - while remaining vigilant about their risks.

7.5. Ubiquitous Public Surveillance: A Double-edged Sword

As public blockchain networks continue to grow, they will capture an increasing number of transactions and interactions. This could create a detailed, immutable record of a significant part of individuals' lives.

In some aspects, the increasing use of blockchain could lead to an unparalleled level of transparency. For instance, it could combat corruption or enforce accountability in public affairs. However, this same transparency could become a tool for ubiquitous public surveillance if unchecked.

7.6. Reflecting on the Future

While blockchain technology holds transformative potential for digitally defining privacy, the future is still being written. For the full potential of blockchain to be realized, individuals, societies, and lawmakers need a significant shift in understanding and approach to data ownership, transactional privacy, and principles of consent.

As conversations around blockchain continue and become deeper and more nuanced, understanding the importance and intricacies of technologies like this - and the paradigms they disrupt, both societal and technological - will be central to navigating our shared future.

In conclusion, the journey towards understanding blockchain is as much about understanding the technology itself as it is about reimagining our societal structures and reevaluating our norms. By offering newfound prospects to redefine and reclaim privacy, blockchain poses both challenges and opportunities. As we move forward, knowledge, understanding, and adaptability will be our best assets. And perhaps, in this journey, we may find that the power to change the rules of privacy has been given back - in some decentralized measure - to the individual.

Chapter 8. Creating Equitable Economies: Blockchain and Financial Inclusion

Given the decentralization at the heart of its design, blockchain presents a promising path to creating equitable economies, transforming the financial systems in ways that can foster inclusion. This potential of blockchain isn't mere speculation; it's backed by compelling innovative initiatives that have already begun to widen access to financial platforms and services.

8.1. Blockchain: A Quick Overview

Before venturing into the nitty-gritty of blockchain's potential for financial inclusion, a basic understanding of the technology is a prerequisite. At its core, blockchain is a distributed ledger technology (DLT) that securely records transactions across a peer-to-peer network. It's designed to be transparent, immutable, and highly secure, which can minimize fraud and lower the need for intermediation, thus reducing costs.

8.2. The Need for Financial Inclusion

It's estimated that nearly 1.7 billion adults globally do not have an account at a financial institution or through a mobile money provider, according to the World Bank. Financial exclusion is a multifaceted dilemma that requires addressing infrastructure challenges, fluctuating income levels, economic instability, and discriminatory policies. However, the advent of blockchain technology has presented an unconventional, tech-driven approach to augment financial inclusion.

8.3. Tackling Exclusion with Blockchain

Blockchain can streamline the financial inclusion process via several avenues. By creating a decentralized digital identity, it assists in overcoming the identification barriers preventing many around the world from accessing financial services. These decentralized identities are secure, portable, and personal, eliminating hurdles like the need for physical documents or biometric data.

Blockchain's peer-to-peer architecture also allows for direct, global financial transactions, effectively reducing or eliminating the role of intermediaries. This can thus lower transaction costs, making financial services more affordable and accessible for low-income individuals.

Typical banking services and remittance corridors also benefit from blockchain. Traditional remittance systems can be slow, expensive, and unreliable, but with blockchain, transactions are transparent, faster, and come with lower costs. For the vast population of migrant workers and their families who rely on these systems, blockchain's implications are significant.

8.4. Groundbreaking Blockchain Initiatives

Across the globe, there are emerging initiatives that harness the power of blockchain to enhance financial inclusion.

BanQu is a blockchain platform aiming to connect the unbanked to the global economy. The platform creates a digital identity for each user that enables them to have a secure, verifiable economic identity.

BitPesa offers blockchain-based remittance services to African nations. By bypassing traditional remittance barriers, BitPesa provides a faster, cheaper, and more reliable service.

Humaniq seeks to empower the unbanked via a simple, blockchain-based mobile app. The app provides biometric identification, making banking services accessible to those without official documents.

8.5. Remaining Challenges

Although blockchain exhibits vast potential, myriad hurdles still exist, hindering its use in promoting financial inclusion. Inadequate infrastructure, a lack of digital literacy, regulatory issues, and scalability constraints are some of these challenges. Underserved populations often lack reliable access to the internet, making blockchain services mostly unattainable.

Moreover, energy consumption demands of blockchain operations, especially for proof-of-work, are substantial. Until more sustainable models are developed, the environmental impact cannot be ignored.

8.6. Conclusion

The disruptive power of blockchain brings tremendous potential to foster more equitable economies, offering solutions to barriers that have traditionally kept people from accessing financial services. Blockchain's promise for financial inclusion is far-reaching, yet, realizing it will require overcoming substantial hurdles. It necessitates a collaborative approach from policymakers, technologists, and society to harness this potential while mitigating associated risks and challenges.

From assisting in identity verification to transforming remittance services, creating decentralized marketplaces, and empowering the unbanked, blockchain could be a revolutionary force in the push towards global financial inclusion — a fitting testament to technology's potential to serve humanity.

Chapter 9. The Dark Side of Blockchain: Potential Risks and Challenges

Before embarking on a journey of exploration, it is fundamentally important to shed light on the potential obstacles that may emerge. Delving into the vast potential of the blockchain technology, forthwith, we must engage with the challenges and risks associated, rendering a more balanced standpoint and avoiding the pitfall of skewed optimism.

9.1. Decentralization and Accountability

One of the most captivating aspects of blockchain technology lies in its decentralized nature. Instead of a single, central authority possessing power over the ledger, a network of independent nodes maintains and verifies transactions. However, the flip side of this disruptive coin is a potential lack of accountability. If a mistake occurs in a transaction, it is not at all easy to rectify given the immutability of blockchain transactions. Moreover, if a user loses access to their cryptocurrency wallet, for instance, retrieving assets is nearly impossible due to the absence of a central point of authority that could intervene.

9.2. Regulatory Scrutiny and Legal Uncertainty

Blockchain technology intersects with legal and regulatory regimes in unparalleled ways. Its international reach, decentralization, and anonymized transactions raise numerous legal and regulatory questions, disrupting the status quo. Some countries have embraced this technology enthusiastically, while others have banned or restricted it due to concerns over potential misuse. The lack of regulatory clarity and legal uniformity across borders presents a significant obstacle for blockchain-based solutions and businesses, inhibiting wider adoption.

9.3. Energy Consumption

Cryptocurrencies like Bitcoin use a consensus method called proof-of-work (PoW) to validate and add new transactions to the ledger, a process known as mining. PoW demands heavy computational resources, leading to significant energy consumption. Recent studies indicate that the energy required for Bitcoin's blockchain surpasses that of some countries. Sustainable solutions need to be sought, or this could become a potential roadblock to broader acceptance.

9.4. Scalability Issues

As the blockchain network expands with increasing users and transactions, the question of scalability in terms of processing speed and storage becomes more acute. Traditional databases offer fast and efficient data processing capabilities, but blockchain, particularly platforms like Bitcoin and Ethereum, suffers from slow transaction processing times and high fees during peak usage - a factor that might limit future growth and adoption.

9.5. Security Concerns

While blockchain's decentralized and immutable nature offers robust security advantages, it is not impervious to attacks. The infamous 51% attack, where a user or a group of users control more than half of a blockchain network's mining power, can disrupt network operations. Similarly, smart contracts, designed to automatically execute transactions upon certain conditions, can also be alluring targets for cybercriminals if not designed and maintained properly.

9.6. Integration Challenges

Finally, for mass adoption of blockchain technology, other systems and businesses must understand and incorporate it. This necessitates both technical understanding and practicality: new software could be needed, more storage may have to be procured, personnel would have to be retrained, and even business models might have to adapt. All of these carry associated costs and complexities, which could slow the transition.

9.7. Conclusion: Balancing Potential with Prudence

As with all technology, blockchain is not immune to challenges and risks. Its revolutionary potential, while exciting, should be matched with a sober examination of potential pitfalls. Decentralization, regulatory scrutiny, energy consumption, scalability, security, and integration challenges represent hurdles that need addressing. As the technology matures and innovative solutions emerge, a careful, balanced understanding of these risks will be instrumental in optimally harnessing blockchain's transformative potential.

Chapter 10. Regulating the Blockchain Revolution: An International Perspective

Blockchain has increasingly come under the lens of regulators worldwide as it ventures bolder into mainstream adoption, changing the way we perceive finance, trust, and individual privacy. Recognizing the transformative potential of this technology while also wary of its disruptive threats, global regulators are striking a careful balance between fostering innovation and mitigating risks. This chapter examines this regulatory landscape from an international perspective, highlighting the varied and evolving responses of major economies, pertinent regulatory issues, and the need for a coordinated international approach.

10.1. The Global Regulatory Landscape

The global regulatory approach to blockchain varies significantly, with different jurisdictions adopting contrasting stances. Some have taken a relaxed and often positive approach to facilitate their growth as blockchain innovation hubs, such as Singapore and Switzerland. Meanwhile, the U.S. and E.U. have adopted more cautious positions, with ongoing explorations and pronouncements on blockchain regulation. On the other hand, countries such as China and India have expressed skepticism and, for a time, instituted outright bans on several blockchain applications.

10.2. Championing Blockchain: Singapore and Switzerland

Singapore's government has consistently expressed support for blockchain. The island nation's regulator, Monetary Authority of Singapore, pursues a robustly pro-active engagement strategy with the sector, directly investing in blockchain ventures through their FinTech Fund. Alongside financial support, Singaporean regulators provide clear, adaptable regulatory frameworks, encouraging blockchain development.

Switzerland, renown as a hub for finance, has also shown support for blockchain technologies. With its 'Crypto Valley' in canton Zug, Switzerland presents lenient regulatory standards, nurturing a thriving blockchain ecosystem. However, as Swiss regulators balance innovation and investor protection, recent legislation increasingly focuses on Anti-Money Laundering (AML) and security issues.

10.3. Cautious Optimism: The U.S. and European Union

In the United States, blockchain regulation is complex due to the division of regulatory authority. Regulators such as the Securities and Exchange Commission (SEC) conduct ongoing examinations of blockchain's potential impacts, particularly focusing on legal definitions of cryptocurrencies, investor protection, and systematic risk.

European Union's approach focuses on research, standard-setting, and development of an integrated market for blockchain services. Comprehensive legislation is expected to come from the E.U.'s Digital Services Act and the European Blockchain Partnership that facilitates an integrated approach focused on potential applications of blockchain in public services and digital identity.

10.4. The Skeptics: China and India

China's stance on blockchain is bifurcated. The Chinese Government vehemently discourages cryptocurrency usage due to financial instability concerns and capital flight risks. In contrast, it is exceedingly proactive regarding the blockchain themselves, encouraging and heavily investing in blockchain projects - but strictly under its control.

India initially banned all cryptocurrency trading in 2018, citing risks associated with AML and terror funding. However, this ban was lifted by the Supreme Court in 2020, citing disproportionate restrictions. Currently, India's regulatory landscape remains uncertain.

10.5. Key Regulatory Issues

In evaluating regulatory responses, four regulatory areas stand out: (1) the legal status of tokens; (2) AML and Counter Terrorist Funding (CTF); (3) Data protection and privacy; and (4) cross-border issues.

Tokens often straddle different legal categories, making it difficult to fit within existing legal frameworks. AML/CTF regulations present unique challenges due to the pseudo-anonymous nature of blockchain transactions. Privacy and data protection in a blockchain context are timely topics given the European General Data Protection Regulation and similarly stringent data protection standards emerging worldwide.

Cross-border issues are highly relevant given the global nature of blockchain's reach. Regulatory arbitrage, where businesses relocate operations to jurisdictions with lighter regulatory requirements, is a particular concern.

10.6. The Need for International Standards

International cooperation is crucial to addressing these regulatory challenges. Considering the inherent cross-border nature of blockchain technology and potential regulatory arbitrage, unilateral regulatory measures risk being ineffective. Major global regulatory bodies such as the International Organization of Securities Commissions (IOSCO) and the Financial Action Task Force (FATF) are hence pivotal in setting international standards for national regulators to implement.

Creating a unified, open regulatory environment can reduce compliance burdens and foster innovation. Working integratively, regulators can navigate the tension between unyieldingly rigid managerial practices that stifle innovation and excessively liberal regulatory regimes that risk system stability and consumer protection.

Blockchain is a transformative revolution in its formative stages – not unlike the internet in its nascent years. As the technology matures, international regulations need to adapt, walking the fine line between sanctioning misuse and nurturing innovation. Further cooperation, standard setting, and globally coordinated responses are essential to fully harness the creative disruption blockchain promises while offering sufficient safeguards against its risks.

Chapter 11. Looking to the Horizon: Predicting the Future of Blockchain Technology

As we plunge into this profound and expansive exploration, it is important to recognize that the horizon of blockchain technology is as diverse and multi-faceted as the challenges it seeks to address. The potential, we believe, is far-reaching; our predictions span from radical changes in the global financial system to drastic shifts in societal norms. This is not a prognostication exercise, but a journey that equips us with tools to navigate the impending revolution in our society.

11.1. Unleashing the Potential of Blockchain in Finance

Considered the innovation that drove the genesis of Bitcoin, blockchain has successfully demonstrated its capacity in the finance domain. The ability of this technology to foster trust, security, and transparency make it a valuable player in this arena. These attributes contribute to the decentralization of financial systems, an idea gaining traction in both emerging and developed economies.

One can predict, with relative confidence, that blockchain will continue to disrupt areas like payments and remittances, clearing and settlement systems, securities trade lifecycle, as well as fundraising and venture capital. This disruption will be charecterized by a shift towards greater efficiency, cost reduction, and democratization of resources and utilities.

In the near term, we envisage an increased uptake of decentralized cryptocurrencies, compelling banking institutions to adjust both strategy and operations to meet the growing demand. Until now, cryptocurrencies have been viewed as a "fringe" or "alternative" investment, but we foresee a future where they could become mainstream.

However, it is in the realm of Decentralized Finance (DeFi), where blockchain's promise is the most transformative. With the goal of creating an open-source, transparent, and permissionless financial system, DeFi could truly redefine the way we perceive and interact with financial markets.

11.2. Reimagining Governance with Blockchain

Blockchain's another remarkable potential area is governance. The technology, due to its decentralized nature, could radically transform existing structures of power. Blockchain-based voting systems, for instance, could offer high levels of security, privacy, and most importantly, trust in election results.

Additionally, blockchain could bring much-needed transparency to the political funding scene. Cryptographically secure records ensure the credibility of contributions. Moreover, a globally accessible, transparent ledger system could introduce a new level of accountability, allowing citizens and regulators alike to trace political donations back to their source.

At the community level, blockchain could enable innovative models of decentralized autonomous organizations (DAOs). DAOs are essentially organizations run by blockchain-embedded codes and contracts, with community consensus driving decisions. This could lead to more inclusive, democratic, and efficient organizations.

11.3. Blockchain and the Future of Identity

As we look towards the future, one of the most exciting possibilities brought about by blockchain lies in identity management. Distributed ledger technology offers a new paradigm for self-sovereign identity - where individuals have control over their digital identity and the personal information it encompasses.

Blockchain could empower individuals with control over their data, defining who can access it and under what conditions. This not only has profound implications for individuals' privacy and security but also changes the dynamics of power between businesses, governments, and consumers.

11.4. The Long Road Ahead: Challenges and Opportunities

However, the path to this horizon is not devoid of challenges. Gaps in understanding, misaligned regulatory infrastructure, technological limitations, and societal resistance all pose hurdles. Yet, with every challenge comes an opportunity to innovate and grow.

As we move forward, it is important to ensure the technology's ethical use. Blockchain's promise is underpinned by its transparency, immutability, and decentralization - features that could be harnessed not just for good, but also for harmful purposes.

Moreover, regulatory clarity will be central to the advancement of blockchain. Legal definitions and frameworks need to adapt to incorporate this dynamic technology, striking the balance between ensuring protection for individuals and allowing the technology room to grow.

Blockchain is still in its infancy, two decades into the 21st century. Challenges remain, but so do the possibilities. The journey towards the full realization of this technology's potential will be one defined by continuous learning, testing, and adjusting.

As technological advancements persist, so too will the growing influence of blockchain. Its future is not etched into stone, but shaped by the collective input and initiatives of all stakeholders involved. In these exciting times, what remains certain is that this technology has the power to bring about sweeping transformations, many of which we are yet to imagine.